COPYRIGHT NOTICE

All scriptures used in this book are from the New International Version (NIV) and the King James Version (KJV) unless otherwise stated.

This book is not intended as a substitute for clinical or spiritual professional counseling. It should not be treated as such.

Edition: November 2025

ISBN: 979-8-9873414-4-5
Printed in the United States of America

NOTE FROM THE AUTHOR

WELCOME

TO THE WORKBOOK COMPANION OF THE A.I.R. EFFECT

DEAR LEADER,

First, let me affirm something important: you are a leader. Whether or not you hold a formal title or manage a team, the truth remains—your life influences others. The way you show up, rise after difficulty, and walk with intention speaks volumes. And that is leadership in motion.

This workbook was designed not just to help you process The A.I.R. Effect—but to help you embody it. As you journey through the 31 principles in the book, this companion guide will give you space to pause, reflect, engage, and most importantly, apply what you're learning. Because leadership is more than information—it's transformation. It's not just what you know; it's how you live it out.

Each section of this workbook is intentionally crafted to walk alongside the A.I.R. Framework:

Activate: Uncover the truths of who you are and the power of your story.

Impart: Identify the wisdom, gifts, and experiences that others are waiting to receive through you.

Release: Learn to lead with trust, pace, and divine timing—knowing when to step up, speak out, and let go.

You'll find journal prompts, reflection exercises, prayer and declaration spaces, and strategy planning tools. Use this workbook to sit with the principles more deeply. Let it become your personal altar—where identity meets insight and where revelation becomes reality.

I encourage you to give yourself grace as you move through these pages. You don't have to rush. Let the Holy Spirit breathe on what needs to be activated in your heart, and let God meet you in both the stillness and the strategy.

Leadership isn't a straight line—it's a sacred rhythm. And this rhythm begins within.

Ansonya L. Burke

With honor and expectation,
Dr. Ansonya L. Burke
Founder, Eikonic Leadership | Creator of The A.I.R. Effect

WORKBOOK CONTENTS

DAILY DEVOTIONAL PRINCIPLES

Each principle includes:

Scripture Meditation

Ground your leadership in truth

Identity Activation

Affirm who God says you are

Leadership Practice

Reflect and act with purpose

Soul Check-In

Pause to examine your heart

Closing Declaration

Seal truth with your voice

SECTION OVERVIEW

SECTION I: ACTIVATE

PRINCIPLE THEMES:
Identity, Self-Awareness, Inner Alignment

- Law 1 – The Law of Empowerment
- The Law of Identifying Growth Edges
- The Law of Wholeness Over Hustle
- The Law of Visionary Leadership
- The Law of Value Creation
- The Law of Foundational Trust
- The Law of Internal Mastery
- The Law of Objective Evaluation
- The Law of Forward Motion
- The Law of Magnetic Leadership

Principle #1

The Law of Empowerment

"Leadership begins with self-government."

Scripture Meditation

"Let your light so shine before men, that they may see your good works and glorify your Father in heaven."
— Matthew 5:16

Identity Activation

Reflect on who you are becoming as a leader—not just what you're doing.

Start here: *What areas of your life do you struggle to see yourself as a leader? Why?*

Write down 3 affirmations that remind you of your influence, even without a title:

- I am a leader when I...
- My voice carries value because...
- I carry influence in...

Reflection & Journal Prompt

"Empowerment begins with self-awareness."

Prompt:
Think of a recent moment when you empowered someone (or could have).

- What did you do or say?
- How did it feel?
- How did they respond?

Now reflect:
What might shift in your relationships if you focused more on empowering presence rather than perfect performance?

Use the space below to reflect honestly. No filters.

Leadership Practice

Choose one simple action this week to empower someone in your sphere of influence:

- Give someone specific encouragement about their strengths
- Delegate a meaningful task and trust their execution
- Share a piece of your story that models growth through vulnerability
- Other: ______________________________________

Plan it. Do it. Reflect on the result.

Soul Check-Ins

Circle what you are currently experiencing as a leader:

☐ Exhaustion
☐ Hope
☐ Vision
☐ Frustration
☐ Clarity
☐ Overwhelm
☐ Boldness
☐ Fear

What concerns of the heart is God revealing to you in your current state? What do you need to release today to lead with greater ease?

Your Leadership Reminder (Write your own):

Closing Declaration:

"I am empowered, not by status, but by the Spirit within me. I lead from authenticity, not perfection. Today, I lead well—starting with myself."

My Notes

Principle #2

The Law of Identifying Growth Edges

"Let your life—not your title—do the talking."

Scripture Meditation

"I have been crucified with Christ and I no longer live, but Christ lives in me. The life I now live in the body, I live by faith in the Son of God, who loved me and gave himself for me."
— Galatians 2:20

Identity Activation

Before you manage people, build companies, or lead teams—know yourself. Self-discovery is not a luxury; it's a leadership prerequisite.

Prompt: *What are your values? What are your non-negotiables? What energizes you—and what drains you? What patterns keep repeating in your leadership?*

Write down 3 affirmations that remind you of your strength and honors your story, how far you've come:

- I honor my story by...
- My identity carries value because...
- I lead with authenticity by...

Reflection & Journal Prompt

"Eikonic Leaders don't hide their process—they honor it"

Prompt:
Think of a recent moment when you empowered someone through transparency.

- What did you do or say?
- How did it feel?
- How did they respond?

Now reflect:

What might shift in your relationships if you owned your story fully, no sanitizing it, and used it to free others to step into theirs?

Use the space below to reflect honestly. No filters.

Leadership Practice

Choose one simple action this week to empower someone by living *aligned* not not perfect:

- Share how you navigated failure and found a better model.
- Talk about when you almost quit and what kept you going.
- Admit when you got it wrong and what it taught you.
- Other: ______________________________________

Plan it. Do it. Reflect on the result.

Soul Check-Ins

What personal edge is God inviting you to stretch beyond?

□ Fear of failure
□ Settling for "good enough"
□ Avoiding difficult feedback
□ Thinking you've already arrived
□ Refusing help when growth requires support

What concerns of the heart is God revealing to you in your current state?

Your Leadership Reminder:
"Growth starts at the edge of your comfort zone."

Closing Declaration:

"I don't chase approval—I walk in alignment.
I know who I am. I own my journey. I show up with clarity and conviction."

My Notes

Principle #3

The Law of Wholeness Over Hustle

"Rhythm is more sustainable than hustle"

Scripture Meditation

"Better one handful with tranquillity
than two handfuls with toil
and chasing after the wind."
— Ecclesiastes 4:6

Identity Activation

Too many visionary leaders are overwhelmed by the gap between big vision and practical execution. This misalignment leads to missed opportunities, burnout, and broken trust with those they lead.

Prompt: What areas of your life do you struggle with either over-strategizing without movement or leaping into action without a clear roadmap?

Write down 3 affirmations that remind you of your ability to execute in rhythm without mindless hustle:

- I operate in rhythm by...
- My wholeness carries strength because...
- I carry execution in...

Reflection & Journal Prompt

"Stewardship bridges the gap between vision and results"

Prompt:

Think of a powerful moment when you didn't focus on doing more—but doing what matters most, consistently and intentionally

- What did you do or say?
- How did it feel?
- How did others respond?

Now reflect:

What might shift in your relationships if you focused more on value outputs rather than the quantity outputs?

Use the space below to reflect honestly. No filters.

Leadership Practice

Choose one simple action this week to empower your people to do what matters most over chasing numbers:

- Set one goal that aligns with your team's true capacity, not just ambition.
- Delegate a meaningful task and trust their execution.
- Create space for creativity, reflection, and recalibration this week.
- Other: ____

Plan it. Do it. Reflect on the result.

Soul Check-Ins

Where might you be sacrificing peace for productivity?

☐ Performing to earn approval
☐ Overcommitting without boundaries
☐ Numbing instead of nurturing
☐ Dismissing your emotional needs
☐ Using busyness to avoid deeper healing

Your Leadership Reminder:
"Wholeness is sacred. Hustle without healing leads to burnout."

Closing Declaration:

"I declare that I am a leader of strategy, discipline, and alignment. I lead from rhythm, not rush. From strategy, not striving. From identity, not insecurity. What I build will last because it's aligned, refined, and anchored in wisdom."

My Notes

Principle #4

The Law of Visionary Leadership

"Without intentional legacy, your success ends with you"

Scripture Meditation

"I pray that the eyes of your heart may be enlightened in order that you may know the hope to which he has called you, the riches of his glorious inheritance in his holy people,"
— Ephesians 1:18

Identity Activation

Many leaders get stuck in short-term wins and shallow influence. They focus on being impressive rather than being impactful. But influence that doesn't outlive you is incomplete.

Prompt: What areas of your life do you struggle with lack of strategy around mentorship, succession, and generational transfer?

Write down 3 affirmations that remind you of your call to legacy building and casting vision:

- I am building legacy by...
- My success is meaningful because...
- I carry vision in...

Reflection & Journal Prompt

"Transition from merely building empires to building generational impact"

Ask yourself:

Who will carry this when I'm gone? If your answer is unclear, your leadership needs recalibration.

- Do your legacy bearers know the vision?
- How are they being equipped?
- How does it feel to contemplate passing on the torch?

Now reflect:

What might shift in your relationships if you trained your replacement as you lead your current mission?

Use the space below to reflect honestly. No filters.

<u>Leadership Practice</u>

Choose one simple action this week to build up someone in your sphere of influence:

- Start a coaching pipeline or apprenticeship model
- Give away the *why* behind your process, not just the what
- Celebrate someone in your circle who has outgrown you
- Other: ____

Plan it. Do it. Reflect on the result.

Soul Check-Ins

What part of your vision have you been afraid to own?

☐ Sharing your God-given dream aloud
☐ Casting vision with clarity and boldness
☐ Believing that your vision is worthy
☐ Taking consistent steps toward execution
☐ Trusting God to resource what He gave you

Your Leadership Reminder:
"Vision is God-breathed, but leadership makes it walk."

Closing Declaration:

"I declare that I am a legacy-minded leader.
My influence outlives me. My obedience impacts generations.
I don't compete with the future—I prepare it."

My Notes

Principle #5

The Law of Value Creation

"Leaders discern who should walk with them—and in what capacity."

Scripture Meditation

"And David shepherded them with integrity of heart;
with skillful hands he led them."
— Psalm 78:72

Identity Activation

Many leaders sabotage their momentum by mismanaging relationships—surrounding themselves with the wrong people, holding onto expired connections, or expecting loyalty without alignment. Without boundaries, access becomes a liability.

Prompt: What areas of your life do you struggle with confusion of unequal partnerships and unspoken expectations?

Write down 3 affirmations that remind you of your ability to build valuable relationships:

- I add value to others when I...
- My time is sacred because...
- I carry wisdom in...

Reflection & Journal Prompt

"Discernment isn't judgment—it's value alignment."

Prompt:

Think of a recent moment when you had to set clear boundaries with a loved one or member of your team.

- What did you do or say?
- How did it feel?
- How did they respond?

Now reflect:

What might shift in your relationships if you focused more sustaining valuable connections rather than holding on to expired ones?

Use the space below to reflect honestly. No filters.

Leadership Practice

Choose one simple action this week to set emotional, spiritual, and professional boundaries:

- Do a personal survey - evaluate who are the truth-tellers versus the cheerleaders in your circle.
- Create a team building activity to build value.
- Take a day or a half day this week to rest, reflect and reset.
- Other: ______________________________________

Plan it. Do it. Reflect on the result.

Soul Check-Ins

Where might you be underestimating your value or withholding your brilliance?

□ Believing you have nothing unique to offer
□ Waiting for perfection before showing up
□ Dismissing your creative contributions
□ Playing small in spaces you're meant to lead
□ Measuring your worth by applause instead of impact

Your Leadership Reminder:
"True leaders don't just consume—they multiply value."

Closing Declaration:

"I declare that I am a wise steward of relationships.
I attract the right people, release the wrong ones, and walk with those aligned to my purpose. I lead with discernment and set boundaries without guilt."

My Notes

Principle #6

The Law of Foundational Trust

"Trust is the bedrock upon which all successful relationships and organizations are built."

Scripture Meditation

"In everything set them an example by doing what is good. In your teaching show integrity, seriousness"

— Titus 2:7

Identity Activation

Reflect on how you can build more trust and integrity in your sphere of influence.

Prompt: What areas of your life do you struggle to show up with consistency--a foundational pillar for building trust?

Write down 3 affirmations that remind you of your character in cultivating integrity:

- I build integrity when I...
- My influence carries value because...
- I am trustworthy because...

Reflection & Journal Prompt

"Trustworthy leaders create environments where people feel secure and valued."

Prompt:

Think of a recent moment when you chose the path of integrity over personal gain.

- What did you do or say?
- How did it feel?
- How did others respond?

Now reflect:

What might shift in your relationships if you focused more on building consistent processes, safe spaces, and ethical practices into your life?

Use the space below to reflect honestly. No filters.

Leadership Practice

Choose one simple action this week to build more trust in your home, church, team, or community:

- Create a nurturing family night to share honest conversation and supportive feedback.
- Make time to follow-up on a promise you made that you have been delaying.
- Invest extra time this week in someone who could benefit from the extra support.
- Other: ______________________________________

Plan it. Do it. Reflect on the result.

Soul Check-Ins

What's threatening your trust in yourself, others, or God right now?

□ Past betrayals still influencing present decisions
□ Micromanaging instead of delegating
□ Second-guessing God's timing or instructions
□ Projecting mistrust onto your team or partners
□ Withholding transparency out of fear of being hurt

Your Leadership Reminder:
"Trust is the soil where leadership takes root."

Closing Declaration:

"I declare that I am a leader with integrity. I am trustworthy. I create consistency all around me. I confront what doesn't belong in me so I can lead what's assigned to me."

My Notes

Principle #7

The Law of Internal Mastery

"Healing precedes healthy leadership"

Scripture Meditation

"Heal me, Lord, and I will be healed;
save me and I will be saved,
for you are the one I praise."
— Jeremiah 17:14

Identity Activation

Many leaders build public platforms while their private worlds are crumbling. They possess talent, charisma, and vision—but lack emotional regulation, personal boundaries, and spiritual depth. The result? Sabotaged influence, short-lived success, and internal exhaustion masked by external applause.

Prompt: What areas of your life is there a disconnect between who you are publicly and who you are privately?

Write down 3 affirmations that speaks to the healing of your internal world:

- I am a healed by...
- My self mastery carries value because...
- I promote healing in others by...

Reflection & Journal Prompt

"Self-mastery is the foundation of legacy leadership"

Prompt:

Think of a recent moment when you lead by internal conviction not crowd-pleasing.

- What did you do or say?
- How did it feel?
- How did they respond?

Now reflect:

What might shift in your relationships if you lead from a place of wholeness, and your influence flowed from authenticity?

Use the space below to reflect honestly. No filters.

Leadership Practice

Choose one simple action this week to encourage internal mastery in those around you:

- Choose to outwardly forgive someone this week.
- Share a moment of personal healing and development with someone in your circle.
- Set a new boundary this week in an area where you've relied on people pleasing to avoid rejection from your team
- Other: ______________________________

Plan it. Do it. Reflect on the result.

Soul Check-Ins

What internal battle is demanding your surrender and discipline?

□ Emotional reactivity sabotaging your impact
□ Impostor syndrome or self-doubt
□ Lack of spiritual discipline or prayer consistency
□ Unhealed trauma influencing leadership decisions
□ Comparing yourself instead of cultivating yourself

Your Leadership Reminder:
"You can't lead what you haven't mastered within."

Closing Declaration:

I declare that I am whole, healed, and aligned. My identity is rooted in truth—not applause. I lead with integrity, walk in wisdom, and steward influence from a place of personal mastery.

My Notes

Principle #8

The Law of Objective Evaluation

"Wisdom is the ability to see clearly—without the fog of emotion or the pull of ego."

Scripture Meditation

"Let the wise listen and add to their learning, and let the discerning get guidance."

— Proverbs 1:5

Identity Activation

Every leader faces moments that test their judgment. The ability to pause, pray, and perceive clearly is one of the highest forms of maturity. Objectivity doesn't mean being detached—it means being discerning. When your mind is cluttered with personal bias or emotion, your vision becomes blurred.

Take a deep breath and invite the Holy Spirit to show you what is true, not just what feels urgent.

Prompt: *When was the last time emotion or personal bias influenced a decision you made? How could wisdom have shifted your response?*

Write down 3 affirmations that speaks to your ability to think objectively:

• I do not rush to react because...

• My ability to listen deeply carries value because...

• I ask better questions when I...

Reflection & Journal Prompt

"Objective evaluation requires balance—between intuition and analysis, compassion and truth."

Prompt: Write your thoughts and realizations below for each prompt.

- How do I typically make decisions—emotion-first or logic-first?
- Which voices influence me most when I evaluate a situation (fear, faith, people, deadlines)?
- What helps me return to clarity when confusion or pressure rises?

Now reflect:

What might shift in your relationships if you lead from a place of objective evaluation using a balance of intuition and practical analysis?

Use the space below to reflect honestly. No filters.

Leadership Practice

This week, choose one area of your life or leadership that requires clearer evaluation.

Ask yourself:

- Have I sought God's perspective on this decision?
- Have I gathered the right information before responding?
- Have I considered the long-term impact, not just the immediate outcome?
- Other: ____

Plan it. Do it. Reflect on the result.

Soul Check-Ins

Circle what you are practicing this week:

□ Listening before leading
□ Seeking wise counsel
□ Slowing down before deciding
□ Releasing emotional clutter

What emotion do you need to surrender to see clearly?

What truth do you need to embrace to move forward?

Your Leadership Reminder:
"Clarity is not found in noise—it's found in stillness."

Closing Declaration:

Today, I choose to evaluate with wisdom, listen without judgment, and decide with discernment.

My Notes

Principle #9

The Law of Forward Motion

"Momentum is built when obedience meets consistency."

Scripture Meditation

"Forget the former things; do not dwell on the past. See, I am doing a new thing! Now it springs up; do you not perceive it?"
— Isaiah 43:18–19

Identity Activation

Forward motion is not about speed—it's about direction. Every step you take in obedience, no matter how small, moves you closer to purpose. The greatest obstacle to progress isn't failure—it's stagnation. When you stop moving, fear and overthinking take root. But when you move, God meets you in motion.

You were never designed to stay stuck. The Spirit within you is a wind that propels, a breath that revives, and a force that fuels movement toward destiny.

Prompt: *Where have I been hesitant to move forward because of fear, comfort, or uncertainty? What one step can I take today to break stagnation?*

Write down 3 affirmations that remind you that you're a leader in motion:

- I am a faithful leader because...
- My trust in God propels me...
- I activate vision by...

Reflection & Journal Prompt

"Forward motion requires faith, focus, and flexibility."

Prompt:

Think of your current movements.

- What area of my life or leadership needs a fresh push of momentum?
- What "old thing" might I need to release to make room for what's next?
- How does consistency in small actions prepare me for greater opportunities?

Now reflect:

Sometimes, God asks us to move before we see the full map. What might shift in your leadership if you let go of what no longer fits?

Use the space below to reflect honestly. No filters.

Leadership Practice

Forward motion isn't always loud—it's steady. This week, identify one goal or responsibility that's been on pause.

- What's one step I can take today to reignite this assignment?
- Who can I invite to hold me accountable?
- What distractions or doubts need to be silenced so I can move forward?
- Other: ______________________________________

Plan it. Do it. Reflect on the result.

Soul Check-Ins

Circle what resonates most this week:

□ I am releasing the past
□ I am taking small, consistent steps
□ I am trusting God in uncertainty
□ I am choosing progress over perfection

What does "forward" look like for you right now—spiritually, emotionally, or strategically?
What is God asking you to start (or restart) today?

Your Leadership Reminder:
"Your pace doesn't determine your purpose—your persistence does. Every obedient step is progress in God's plan."

Closing Declaration:

I move with grace and purpose. I do not shrink back in fear, nor stay stuck in comfort. The God who called me forward walks with me into every new season. My momentum is divine—steady, strong, and Spirit-led. I am built for progress, aligned with purpose, and anchored in faith. Today, I move forward.

My Notes

Principle #10

The Law of Magnetic Leadership

"Great leadership doesn't demand attention—it draws it through authenticity, vision, and presence."

Scripture Meditation

"Let your light so shine before men, that they may see your good works and glorify your Father in heaven."
— Matthew 5:16 (NKJV)

Identity Activation

Magnetic leaders don't chase influence—they embody it. They lead with clarity, humility, and conviction, and as a result, people are naturally drawn to their presence. But here's the secret: magnetic leadership begins within. When your identity is rooted in Christ, your confidence is contagious. Your authenticity becomes your strongest attraction.

This law isn't about charisma—it's about alignment. What draws others to you is not your volume, but your vibration—the resonance of a life lived in purpose.

Prompt: *What do people naturally come to you for (wisdom, peace, direction, inspiration)? What might that reveal about your God-given leadership "pull"?*

Write down 3 affirmations that remind you that you're a magnetic leader, even without a title:

- I draw people to me by...

- My presence carries value because...

- My integrity is magnetic because...

Reflection & Journal Prompt

"Leadership that magnetizes others is cultivated through presence and integrity."

Questions to ponder:

- Am I fully present in the spaces where I lead, or am I rushing through moments?
- Do others feel seen, heard, and valued in my presence?
- What part of my leadership feels forced—and what flows naturally?

Now reflect:

What might shift in your relationships if you practiced magnetic presence—fully engaged, non-performative, authentic leadership?

Use the space below to reflect honestly. No filters.

Leadership Practice

This week, become a student of your own presence. Ask a trusted peer, friend, or colleague:

- "What is it about my leadership that draws you in?"

Listen to their response without defensiveness. Then take a moment to answer for yourself:

- *What would it look like for me to lead with less pressure and more presence?*

Plan it. Do it. Reflect on the result.

Soul Check-Ins

Circle one area to lean into this week:

□ Authenticity over image
□ Influence over control
□ Presence over performance
□ Clarity over confusion

In one word, how do you want others to feel after interacting with your leadership this week?
What distractions or insecurities might you need to lay down to embody that?

Your Leadership Reminder:
"What you carry inwardly becomes what people feel outwardly. Lead from your overflow, not your performance."

Closing Declaration:

"I don't lead from insecurity—I lead from identity.
I don't hustle for approval—I rest in divine affirmation and my God-given authentic natural pull."

My Notes

SECTION II: IMPART

PRINCIPLE THEMES:

Strategy, People Leadership, Communication, Culture

- The Law of Genuine Connection
- The Law of Selfless Leadership
- The Law of Dynamic Systems
- The Law of Freedom Through Forgiveness
- The Law of Exponential Growth
- The Law of Exemplary Leadership
- The Law of Insightful Leadership
- The Law of Multiplication Through Mentorship
- The Law of Empowered Leadership
- The Law of Excellence in Details
- The Law of Compounding Impact

Principle #11

The Law of Genuine Connection

"Leadership without connection is simply direction without impact."

Scripture Meditation

"Let love be genuine. Abhor what is evil; hold fast to what is good. Love one another with brotherly affection. Outdo one another in showing honor."

— Romans 12:9–10 (ESV)

Identity Activation

Connection is at the heart of transformative leadership. Genuine connection doesn't come from a title—it flows from authenticity, emotional availability, and a commitment to truly see others.

Whether you're leading in a boardroom, classroom, sanctuary, or home, people are drawn to leaders who connect with compassion and care—not just with direction.

To lead with genuine connection means to listen with empathy, respond with kindness, and build trust through presence.

Prompt: *Think of someone who leads with heart and connection. What do they do differently? How do they make others feel?*

Write down 3 affirmations that you lead with genuine connection:

- I lead genuinely when I...

- My connections carry depth because...

- I am a trustworthy leader because...

Reflection & Journal Prompt

"Many people follow out of obligation. Few follow out of trust."

Prompt:

Think about your current leadership style and connections.

- Do I allow space for vulnerability in my leadership?
- When was the last time I truly checked in on someone's heart—not just their performance?
- Am I showing up with warmth, or simply giving instructions?

Now reflect:

Connection breaks through the walls of hierarchy and fear. What might shift in your relationships if you invited people into a safer collaborative environment?

Use the space below to reflect honestly. No filters.

Leadership Practice

This week, choose one person you lead or influence and intentionally connect with them beyond the task at hand.

- Ask, "How are you doing?" and wait for the honest answer.

Listen—not to fix, but to understand. Show up not as a role, but as a real human.

Plan it. Do it. Reflect on the result.

Soul Check-Ins

Circle one area where you desire deeper connection this week:

□ My team or coworkers
□ My ministry or spiritual community
□ My family
□ Myself (self-connection)

What's one thing I can do to nurture connection in that space this week?

Your Leadership Reminder:
"People may forget your words, but they will remember how your presence made them feel safe, seen, and valued."

Closing Declaration:

I lead with love, not just logic. I connect deeply. My leadership flows from authenticity, and those I lead feel the warmth of my intention, the safety of my presence, and the strength of our bond. I do not lead alone—I lead with God, and I lead with heart.

My Notes

Principle #12

The Law of Selfless Leadership

"True greatness is measured not by how much you gain, but by how much you give."

Scripture Meditation

"Do nothing out of selfish ambition or vain conceit. Rather, in humility value others above yourselves."
— Philippians 2:3

Identity Activation

Selfless leadership is not weakness—it is strength under control. It's leading with open hands instead of closed fists. When you lead selflessly, you exchange ego for empathy, competition for collaboration, and recognition for responsibility.

The world often rewards leaders for what they achieve, but Heaven celebrates leaders for what they release—the encouragement, opportunities, and wisdom they pour into others.

Prompt: *Who in your life has modeled selfless leadership? What specific qualities made their leadership different?*

Write down 3 affirmations that remind you of your influence, even without a title:

- I am a selfless leader...
- My empathy demonstrates...
- I empower others by...

Reflection & Journal Prompt

"The selfless leader doesn't lead to be seen—they lead so others can see."

Prompt:

Think of intently on these common leadership pitfalls.

- When was the last time I served without seeking credit or praise?
- How can I shift my focus from personal success to collective growth?
- Where might pride or fear be preventing me from serving freely?

Now reflect:

What might shift in your relationships if you focused on building people, not platforms?

Use the space below to reflect honestly. No filters.

Leadership Practice

This week, practice invisible leadership. Do one act of service or generosity for someone you lead or work alongside—without announcing it or expecting thanks.

- Who needs encouragement right now?
- Where can I lighten someone's load today?
- How can I lead through serving instead of striving?
- Other: ______________________________________

Plan it. Do it. Reflect on the result.

Soul Check-Ins

Circle what resonates most this week:

□ I am learning to serve from strength, not scarcity
□ I am leading with humility and empathy
□ I am releasing my need for recognition
□ I am honoring others above myself

What shifts in your heart when you stop leading for applause and start leading from assignment?
What does servant leadership look like in your current season?

Your Leadership Reminder:
"You don't lose your power when you serve—you reveal it."

Closing Declaration:

I lead with humility and strength. My leadership reflects the heart of service, not self-promotion. My influence is multiplied through generosity, compassion, and grace. I am not striving to be noticed—I am positioned to make an eternal impact. I lead selflessly, and I lead well.

My Notes

Principle #13

The Law of Dynamic Systems

"Leadership isn't static—it must flow, shift, and evolve in sync with divine movement."

Scripture Meditation

"See, I am doing a new thing! Now it springs up; do you not perceive it? I am making a way in the wilderness and streams in the wasteland."

— Isaiah 43:19

Identity Activation

Dynamic systems are living, breathing ecosystems—ever-changing, always adapting. As a leader, your spiritual system must be flexible enough to expand with divine revelation and structured enough to support transformation. Stagnant leadership resists movement, but dynamic leadership embraces the flow of growth, learning, and divine recalibration.

The Law of Dynamic Systems reminds you that what worked before may not be what is needed now. Are you willing to evolve?

Prompt: *What area of your leadership has grown too comfortable, too fixed? What sacred systems might God be inviting you to rebuild?*

Write down 3 affirmations that speak to your ability to shift and pivot when needed:

- I am a growth leader...
- My flexibility speaks to...
- I accept new shifts by...

Reflection & Journal Prompt

"God's systems are never aimless—they are purposeful, strategic, and season-specific."

Prompt:

Think of a recent moment when you positioned yourself to flow with grace rather than grind from strain.

- Where in your leadership have you mistaken structure for control?
- How open are you to letting go of outdated methods or models?
- What would it look like for your leadership to function like a Spirit-led ecosystem?

Now reflect:

What might shift in your relationships if you operated by the law of dynamic systems, you aligned your internal rhythms with divine direction?

Use the space below to reflect honestly. No filters.

Leadership Practice

This week, evaluate your systems—spiritual, strategic, relational. Are they producing life? Are they still aligned with your current assignment? Make one intentional change to increase alignment, not efficiency alone.

- Is this system still serving my mission or just my comfort?
- What feedback have I been ignoring from those I lead?
- Am I making room for God to shift the strategy?

Plan it. Do it. Reflect on the result.

Soul Check-Ins

Circle what resonates most this week:

□ I am being invited into a new rhythm
□ I will not idolize old systems
□ I embrace change as a divine invitation
□ I trust God to re-structure what feels unstable

What new system is the Holy Spirit birthing in this season of your leadership? What needs to be dismantled before it can be rebuilt?

Your Leadership Reminder:
"Dynamic systems lead to dynamic impact. Let your structure serve the Spirit—not the other way around."

Closing Declaration:

I am aligned with divine flow. My leadership is flexible, faithful, and ready for renewal. I release outdated systems and embrace fresh strategies. I lead with structure—but never at the cost of movement. I am a dynamic leader, led by a dynamic God.

My Notes

Principle #14

The Law of Freedom Through Forgiveness

"Forgiveness is the gatekeeper of freedom. What you don't release, rules you."

Scripture Meditation

"Be kind and compassionate to one another, forgiving each other, just as in Christ God forgave you."
— Ephesians 4:32

Identity Activation

Forgiveness is not weakness—it is a spiritual strategy that dismantles bitterness, pride, and emotional stagnation. Leaders who refuse to forgive stay tethered to the offenses of the past, unable to fully step into the future. To lead with clarity, peace, and wisdom, you must first release what's weighing you down. Forgiveness does not mean agreeing with injustice. It means you are choosing freedom over bondage and future over fixation.

Prompt: *Who do you need to forgive in order to lead from wholeness?*
Is it someone else—or yourself?

Write down 3 affirmations that help you release offense and walk in forgiveness as a leader:

- I release myself from...
- I choose to forgive because...
- Freedom allows me to...

Reflection & Journal Prompt

"Forgiveness is not a one-time event; it's a continual decision to live unbound."

Prompt:

A free leader is a powerful leader—because freedom brings clarity, humility, and compassion.

- How has unforgiveness affected my peace, creativity, or relationships?
- What have I gained by holding onto pain—and what could I gain by releasing it?
- What does walking in daily forgiveness look like for me as a leader?

Now reflect:

What might shift in your relationships if you forgave and reclaimed emotional territory the enemy once occupied?

Use the space below to reflect honestly. No filters.

Leadership Practice

Forgiveness restores flow. This week, ask the Holy Spirit to bring one person or memory to mind that still holds emotional charge. Pray over it—not for validation, but for release.

- Have I made peace with this situation, or just buried it?
- What lesson is God trying to teach me through this pain?
- How can I lead with compassion without carrying the offense?

Plan it. Do it. Reflect on the result.

Soul Check-Ins

Circle what resonates most this week:

□ I choose peace over pride
□ I release what no longer serves me
□ I forgive to protect my purpose
□ I am no longer bound by bitterness

What freedom feels overdue in your life right now?
How can forgiving yourself unlock greater leadership clarity?

Your Leadership Reminder:
"Forgiveness doesn't erase the past—it redeems it."

Closing Declaration:

I am a leader who forgives quickly and fully. I release all resentment, guilt, and offense that no longer serves my growth. I am free to lead with joy, to love without limits, and to live unbound. My heart is healed, my mind is renewed, and my leadership flows from a place of grace.

My Notes

Principle #15

The Law of Exponential Growth

"Growth is not just addition—it's multiplication when rooted in alignment and legacy."

Scripture Meditation

"The Kingdom of Heaven is like a mustard seed... though it is the smallest of all seeds, yet when it grows, it is the largest of garden plants and becomes a tree."

— Matthew 13:31–32

Identity Activation

Exponential growth begins within. It doesn't start with platforms or promotions—it starts with alignment, stewardship, and obedience. The seed in your hand may seem small, but it contains legacy within its DNA. When you cultivate your spiritual and leadership disciplines consistently, God breathes on your obedience and causes it to multiply in ways you couldn't manufacture.

Growth becomes exponential when you're not just building for yourself, but investing in others. As you activate others, impart wisdom, and release your influence with humility and intention, your impact extends far beyond your own reach.

Prompt: *Where in your life or leadership are you seeing signs of multiplication? Where might you be resisting growth that requires greater responsibility?*

Write down 3 affirmations to anchor your faith in what God is multiplying through your leadership:

- Even small seeds can grow into...
- I am stewarding what God gave me by...
- Multiplication will come when I...

Reflection & Journal Prompt

"True growth requires pruning, obedience, and releasing control of outcomes."

Prompt:

Sometimes growth doesn't look exponential because we're measuring it through human metrics.

- Where have I seen growth that didn't come from striving?
- What systems or habits can I implement to support consistent growth?
- Who in my life or team am I being called to mentor, activate, or release?

Now reflect:

What might shift in your leadership is you allowed God to expand you in unseen, eternal ways?

Use the space below to reflect honestly. No filters.

Leadership Practice

Exponential growth is not about doing more—it's about doing what matters most.

This week, take inventory of where your time, energy, and focus are going. Are you sowing into activities that bear fruit—or just motion?

- Track your weekly leadership actions.
- Identify one area to eliminate or delegate.
- Choose one person to intentionally invest in (pray, encourage, pour into).

Plan it. Do it. Reflect on the result.

Soul Check-Ins

Circle what speaks to you most:

□ I believe small seeds can grow big things
□ I choose faith over fear in seasons of stretch
□ I am being expanded, not overwhelmed
□ I am committed to lasting, multiplying impact

What's one way you can create a system that multiplies your impact this month?
What does "kingdom-centered growth" look like for you in this season?

Your Leadership Reminder:
"You don't grow by doing more—you grow by doing what matters with clarity and consistency."

Closing Declaration:

I am a vessel of multiplying impact. I sow in faith, I serve in obedience, and I lead with intention. I believe God is expanding my influence beyond what I can see. I am growing—deep, wide, and lasting.

My Notes

Principle #16

The Law of Exemplary Leadership

"True leadership isn't declared—it's demonstrated."

Scripture Meditation

"In everything set them an example by doing what is good. In your teaching show integrity, seriousness and soundness of speech that cannot be condemned..."

— Titus 2:7–8

Identity Activation

Exemplary leadership is not about perfection—it's about consistency, integrity, and authenticity. Leaders who live what they teach lead with credibility. People follow what they see more than what they hear, and when your actions align with your message, you cultivate trust, influence, and impact.

You don't need a spotlight to lead by example. Whether in your home, workplace, ministry, or online presence, your consistency creates a legacy. Exemplary leaders show up even when it's inconvenient, choose excellence when no one is watching, and honor their calling through discipline and discernment.

Prompt: *Where is your leadership silently speaking volumes? What behaviors are you modeling for others?*

Write down 3 affirmations that ground you in the power of leadership by example:

- I lead with integrity when I...

- My lifestyle preaches by...

- People can trust my leadership because...

Reflection & Journal Prompt

"Your consistency is preaching even when your mouth is closed."

Prompt:

We often think leadership is about big speeches or bold moves, but it's often shaped by the small, daily choices.

- What values am I modeling through my leadership presence?
- Where might my lifestyle need to catch up with my message?
- Who around me is quietly watching and being shaped by my example?

Now reflect:

What might shift in your relationships if you focused more aligning your lifestyle with God's word?

Use the space below to reflect honestly. No filters.

Leadership Practice

This week, pick one leadership value (such as excellence, humility, or accountability) and intentionally practice it in both public and private spaces.

Then, notice how people respond—not just to your words, but to your walk.

- Choose a leadership value to embody this week.
- Create a "mirror moment" checklist to self-assess before each major interaction.
- Invite someone you trust to hold you accountable in private to what you profess in public.

Plan it. Do it. Reflect on the result.

Soul Check-Ins

Circle what speaks to you most:

□ I lead from example, not ego
□ My integrity matters even in hidden places
□ I am a model of consistency and clarity
□ My lifestyle speaks louder than my platform

What does it look like to lead "with your life" in this season?
What small leadership habit can you recommit to today?

Your Leadership Reminder:
"Don't just say it—live it. Your consistency will do more for others than your charisma ever could."

Closing Declaration:

I am an exemplary leader. I lead with discipline, live with integrity, and model what I believe. I honor the assignment on my life with consistency and excellence. I understand that leadership begins within and shows up in how I treat others, how I respond under pressure, and how I reflect the heart of God. My life is my message —and I lead it well.

My Notes

Principle #17

The Law of Insightful Leadership

"Wisdom is not just knowing more—it's discerning what truly matters."

Scripture Meditation

Wisdom is the principal thing;
Therefore get wisdom.
And in all your getting, get understanding.
— Proverbs 4:7 (NKJV)

Identity Activation

Insightful leaders don't just react—they reflect. They move beyond surface-level decisions and tap into spiritual discernment, emotional intelligence, and godly wisdom to lead with precision and purpose. Their leadership isn't loud—but it is deep, rooted, and profoundly transformational.

Insightful leadership is about asking the right questions, not just having all the answers. It's about pausing to seek God's heart, interpreting the unseen, and discerning the difference between good and God. In a world obsessed with speed and visibility, you are called to be a leader of depth—one who listens more than speaks and sees beyond what's obvious.

Prompt: *Where has insight guided you more powerfully than information alone? What wisdom do you need to seek in this current season?*

Write down 3 affirmations that anchor you in your calling as an insightful leader:

- I lead with insight when I...
- God grants me wisdom to...
- My discernment grows as I...

Reflection & Journal Prompt

"In seasons of growth, transition, or confusion, insight becomes your compass."

Prompt:

Insight is cultivated through intimacy with God, quiet reflection, and a commitment to not lead in haste.

- How do you create space to hear divine insight before acting?
- Where do you need wisdom instead of answers right now?
- What distractions may be blocking your ability to perceive clearly?

Now reflect:

What might shift in your pivotal leadership moments if you relied on not just quick thinking—but quiet knowing?

Use the space below to reflect honestly. No filters.

Leadership Practice

This week, practice slowing down to listen. Before making a decision—pause, pray, and journal. Whether it's a business meeting, ministry direction, or personal challenge, choose to respond rather than react.

- Schedule a 15-minute "wisdom check-in" at the start or end of each day.

- Create an "insight journal" entry for 3 key areas of your leadership.

- Ask God, "What am I not seeing that You want to reveal?"

Plan it. Do it. Reflect on the result.

Soul Check-Ins

Circle what speaks to you most:

□ I am a leader of wisdom and weight
□ My insight deepens through intimacy with God
□ I ask questions before offering answers
□ Discernment is one of my greatest tools

In what area of your leadership do you need divine insight today?
What old patterns are you ready to release to lead more clearly?

Your Leadership Reminder:
"Insightful leadership isn't about controlling everything—it's about perceiving the right things and moving in God's timing."

Closing Declaration:

I lead with insight, not impulse. I carry discernment that comes from my relationship with God. I listen before I speak, I observe before I decide, and I seek wisdom over applause. My insight creates safe spaces for others, sets the tone for wise leadership, and allows me to respond with clarity, compassion, and confidence. I am not led by pressure—I am anchored in purpose.

My Notes

Principle #18

The Law of Multiplication Through Mentorship

"You grow when you invest in others—your leadership legacy is not what you build alone, but who you build up."

Scripture Meditation

"And the things you have heard me say in the presence of many witnesses entrust to reliable people who will also be qualified to teach others."

— 2 Timothy 2:2

Identity Activation

The most effective leaders understand that leadership isn't about personal success—it's about multiplying impact through intentional mentorship. It's not enough to be gifted, called, or successful if no one else is growing because of your presence. Legacy requires you to pour into others with intentionality.

Multiplication begins when you recognize the divine weight of your influence. Whether you're mentoring a team, a younger peer, your children, or a small group at church, your leadership deepens every time you sow your wisdom into others. Your story, scars, and strategies are seeds that can empower someone else's breakthrough.

Prompt: *Who are you currently pouring into? Who once believed in you and helped shape who you are?*

Write down 3 affirmations that remind you how God uses you to multiply impact through mentorship:

- I multiply leadership when I...

- Others grow because I choose to...

- My voice plants seeds of...

Reflection & Journal Prompt

"You don't need a title or platform to mentor someone—you just need willingness."

Prompt:

Multiplication doesn't happen by chance; it's the result of intentional guidance, nurturing conversations, and showing up when it matters.

- Who are 1–2 people you can intentionally mentor in this season?
- What core lesson have you learned that you can pass on?
- What legacy are you building beyond your own success?

Now reflect:

What might shift in your sphere of influence if used your lived experiences, leadership journey, and God-given insight as tools for someone else's growth?

Use the space below to reflect honestly. No filters.

Leadership Practice

This week, practice legacy leadership through mentorship. Reach out to someone who needs your wisdom, encouragement, or presence—even if informally.

- Write a note or text of encouragement to someone in their early leadership journey.
- Offer to pray with or coach someone who reminds you of where you once were.
- Create a short list of 2–3 key leadership lessons you want to intentionally pass on.

Plan it. Do it. Reflect on the result.

Soul Check-Ins

Circle what resonates most with your leadership today:

□ I'm committed to building legacy through mentorship
□ I believe my leadership multiplies through others
□ I carry wisdom worth passing on
□ I am an answer to someone else's prayer for guidance

What does kingdom multiplication look like for you right now?
What small step can you take to sow into someone else's growth?

Your Leadership Reminder:
"Leadership is not just about rising—it's about raising others up. Mentorship is the bridge between your impact today and your legacy tomorrow."

Closing Declaration:

I am a leader who multiplies. I pour out what I've learned, freely and faithfully. I lead with legacy in mind. I believe in raising up others with grace, truth, and intentionality. My impact is not measured by what I do alone but by the leaders I help activate. Through mentorship, I release a ripple of influence that echoes beyond me.

My Notes

Principle #19

The Law of Empowered Leadership

"Strong leaders don't shrink others—they strengthen them."

Scripture Meditation

"Therefore encourage one another and build one another up, just as you are doing."
— 1 Thessalonians 5:11 (ESV)

Identity Activation

Empowered leaders are secure in their identity. They don't lead from comparison or fear but from confidence in the One who called them. When you understand that your assignment is unique and your value is anchored in God, you're no longer threatened by someone else's growth—you celebrate it.

This law reminds us that power is not a possession—it's a responsibility. As leaders, we're called to build others up, to affirm their strengths, to share the platform, and to make room at the table. True leadership is not proven in what you accomplish alone but in how you equip and uplift others.

Prompt: *What does empowered leadership look like in your daily life? Are you creating opportunities for others to grow?*

Write down 3 affirmations that anchor your identity as an empowering leader:

- I lift others by...
- I lead with strength that...
- I create room for others to...

Reflection & Journal Prompt

"Sometimes, the most empowering thing a leader can do is speak life."

Prompt:

Empowered leadership is humble, discerning, and generous—it doesn't hoard influence, it multiplies it.

- Who in your circle needs your encouragement today?
- Have you ever withheld support out of fear or insecurity? What did that moment teach you?
- How can you intentionally raise up the next leader this week?

Now reflect:

What might shift in your relationships if you stepped aside so someone close to you could shine?

Use the space below to reflect honestly. No filters.

Leadership Practice

This week, empower intentionally.

- Identify someone whose leadership potential you admire but hasn't yet been affirmed. Speak into their potential.
- Delegate an opportunity to someone else and celebrate their success—even if you could've done it yourself.
- Share a resource, connection, or platform that could help someone else grow.

Plan it. Do it. Reflect on the result.

Soul Check-Ins

Which of these resonates with your current season of leadership?

□ I want to empower others with confidence, not fear
□ I recognize that my influence can multiply others
□ I am committed to building up—not tearing down
□ I believe there's room for all of us to rise

What does a legacy of empowerment look like to you?

Your Leadership Reminder:
"Empowered leaders don't compete with others—they complete the mission through others."

Closing Declaration:

I lead from abundance, not scarcity. I believe in the power of shared influence. I release comparison and choose to honor the gifts in others. My leadership multiplies because I choose to speak life, open doors, and build people. I am not intimidated by greatness—I ignite it.

My Notes

Principle #20

The Law of Excellence in Details

"Excellence is not about perfection—it's about intention."

Scripture Meditation

"Whatever you do, work at it with all your heart, as working for the Lord, not for human masters."
— Colossians 3:23

Identity Activation

You weren't created for mediocrity. The Spirit of God within you equips you to lead with excellence—not just in the big, visible moments, but in the hidden details no one sees. The Law of Excellence in Details reminds us that how we do something matters just as much as what we do. God honors precision, care, and follow-through.

As a leader, your attention to detail reflects your stewardship. Whether it's preparing for a meeting, creating a project plan, leading a worship service, or writing an email—how you carry it speaks volumes. You don't have to be flashy. You just have to be faithful.

Prompt: *Do I consistently honor God through my excellence, even when no one is watching? What "small things" in my leadership practice need more intentional care?*

Write down 3 affirmations that remind you that excellence starts in the unseen:

- I honor God by...
- My excellence reveals...
- Even the smallest details matter because...

Reflection & Journal Prompt

"Excellence is not about striving—it's about intentionality."

Prompt:

When we're intentional with our time, our preparation, and our follow-through, we create an environment of trust, reliability, and honor.

- Where have I allowed "good enough" to replace God-honoring excellence?

- What routines or systems can I build to elevate the details in my work or ministry?

- What does a spirit of excellence look like in my home, relationships, or leadership?

Now reflect:

What might shift in your relationships if you paid more attention to the details when supporting others?

Use the space below to reflect honestly. No filters.

Leadership Practice
This week, examine the details.

- Review one task or project and improve it by 5–10%.
- Ask someone you trust to give you honest feedback on the small things you may overlook.
- Choose to go above and beyond in one area others might consider "minor."
- Other: ____

Plan it. Do it. Reflect on the result.

Soul Check-Ins
Which of these feels most true for this season?

□ I desire to bring God glory in the details
□ I sometimes overlook small things in the rush to finish
□ I am committed to consistency, not just convenience
□ I believe excellence is a reflection of spiritual maturity

Where is God inviting you to raise the standard?

Your Leadership Reminder:
"Excellence is not about applause. It's about alignment—with your assignment and with the Spirit of God."

Closing Declaration:

"I lead with intention. I steward the small things with care. My attention to detail reflects my dedication to the One who called me. I choose excellence in every season—visible or hidden. I rise above mediocrity and embrace the divine discipline of excellence.

My Notes

Principle #21

The Law of Compounding Impact

"Small seeds, when sown consistently, yield supernatural harvests."

Scripture Meditation

"So let's not get tired of doing what is good. At just the right time we will reap a harvest of blessing if we don't give up."
— Galatians 6:9 (NLT)

Identity Activation

Impact doesn't always come in loud bursts or overnight miracles. Often, it builds slowly—layer by layer, day by day. The Law of Compounding Impact reminds you that faithfulness over time leads to exponential influence. Every act of obedience, every small yes, every quiet moment of service—it all matters.

You may not see results immediately, but the fruit is forming beneath the surface. Leaders who understand this law are not easily discouraged. They trust God's timing and remain diligent in planting, watering, and stewarding what they've been given.

Prompt: *What seeds am I sowing today that align with my long-term vision? How can I remain consistent even when results are not immediate?*

Write down 3 affirmations that remind you of your long-term impact and divine consistency:

- I am building legacy by...
- God honors my consistency, even when...
- My influence expands when I...

Reflection & Journal Prompt

"Leaders who steward the small things faithfully over time see massive results others miss."

Prompt:

Compounding impact is about consistent obedience, strategic patience, and the faith to believe that your leadership matters—today and beyond.

- Have I been underestimating the power of daily obedience?
- Where have I abandoned a seed too early because I didn't see instant growth?
- What's one habit or practice I can recommit to that will multiply my impact over time?

Now reflect:

How might your leadership evolve if you focused more on the areas where you face challenges?

Use the space below to reflect honestly. No filters.

Leadership Practice

This week, track your compound actions.

- Identify one small action to do consistently (daily or weekly).
- Document what you learn, how you feel, and how it affects others.
- Celebrate consistency over perfection.
- Other: ______________________________________

Plan it. Do it. Reflect on the result.

Soul Check-Ins

Which of these truths resonates most right now?

□ I am sowing into something bigger than myself
□ My leadership is a daily investment
□ I choose consistency, even when it's unseen
□ My obedience will outlast opposition

What "impact" looks like may change—but the process remains the same.

Your Leadership Reminder:
"Kingdom impact grows silently, steadily, and supernaturally when we remain faithful in the small things."

Closing Declaration:

I am a cultivator of impact. I lead with intention and show up in excellence, even when no one is watching. I trust God to multiply my obedience, and I believe that every step I take in purpose brings exponential growth to my legacy. I will not grow weary—I will grow deeper.

My Notes

SECTION III: RELEASE

PRINCIPLE THEMES:
Legacy, Succession, Expansion, Spiritual Authority

- The Law of Unified Triumph
- The Law of Purposeful Priorities
- The Law of Accountable Leadership
- The Law of Creative Leadership
- The Law of Visionary Execution
- The Law of Empowered Belief
- The Law of Courageous Communication
- The Law of Mutual Growth
- The Law of Authentic Acceptance
- The Law of Empowering Embrace

Principle #22

The Law of Unified Triumph

"Victory is multiplied when we move together in unity, not competition."

Scripture Meditation

"How good and pleasant it is when God's people live together in unity!... For there the Lord bestows His blessing, even life forevermore."

— Psalm 133:1, 3

Identity Activation

Leadership that isolates will eventually fracture. Leadership that unifies will flourish. The Law of Unified Triumph teaches that true success is not a solo mission—it's a collective assignment. God designed Kingdom leadership to operate in partnership, alignment, and mutual honor.

When you reject comparison and competition, you make room for divine collaboration. Whether you lead a team, serve in ministry, or steward influence in your home or community, the victories you're called to walk in are communal, not isolated.

Prompt: *Where have I been trying to lead alone when God has called me to build together? What partnerships or relationships has God given me that I need to steward better?*

Write down 3 affirmations that root your leadership in unity and shared success:

- I honor the gifts of others because...
- I lead best when I collaborate by...
- God increases my impact when I choose...

Reflection & Journal Prompt

"Unity in leadership requires humility, vision, and emotional maturity."

Prompt:

The leaders who thrive are those who can see the strengths in others without shrinking their own identity.

- Do I secretly fear being overshadowed by others' success?
- Have I struggled to build trust-based relationships in leadership?
- How can I shift from "me" to "we" in my leadership style?

Now reflect:

What might shift in your relationships if you focused on building trust-based relationships?

Use the space below to reflect honestly. No filters.

Leadership Practice

This week, practice intentional unity:

- Affirm a team member or peer leader publicly.
- Initiate collaboration on a goal you've been pursuing solo.
- Reflect on how shared leadership multiplies strength—not diminishes it.
- Other: ____

Plan it. Do it. Reflect on the result.

Soul Check-Ins

Which of these truths is God emphasizing for you today?

□ I was never meant to carry the vision alone
□ I can lead with others without losing myself
□ Honor and humility create supernatural synergy
□ Unified triumph honors God more than individual success

Your Leadership Reminder:
"Unity is not uniformity. It's divine agreement in motion—and it unlocks supernatural blessing."

Closing Declaration:

I am a leader who values collaboration. I reject competition, celebrate others, and build with honor. The victories I walk into are not mine alone—they are part of a greater purpose and people. God has connected me to win, together.

My Notes

Principle #23

The Law of Purposeful Priorities

"Great leaders don't do everything. They do the right things, in the right order, for the right reason."

Scripture Meditation

"But seek first His kingdom and His righteousness, and all these things will be given to you as well."
— Matthew 6:33

Identity Activation

Leadership is not about doing more—it's about doing what matters most. The Law of Purposeful Priorities reminds us that when everything is important, nothing truly is. As Kingdom leaders, our assignment is not just to be busy, but to be effective.

When your leadership stems from divine clarity, your priorities reflect your purpose. Distractions decrease. Discernment increases. You no longer chase every opportunity; you align with what heaven has already assigned to you.

Prompt: *What has God called me to focus on in this season? What distractions do I need to release so I can lead with greater clarity?*

Write down 3 affirmations to help you stay rooted in purposeful leadership:

- My time honors God when I...
- I lead with excellence when I prioritize...
- I release what's good so I can pursue...

Reflection & Journal Prompt

"A leader's calendar reflects their convictions."

Prompt:

Every yes comes with a cost—and every no protects your vision. Prioritizing your God-given purpose may require you to disappoint others, but it will never disappoint your destiny.

- What activities are no longer aligned with my assignment?
- Where am I overextended due to unclear boundaries or misplaced urgency?
- How can I restructure my routines to reflect my true priorities?

Now reflect:

How might your relationships change if you began establishing appropriate boundaries regarding your time management?

Use the space below to reflect honestly. No filters.

Leadership Practice

This week, audit your time and energy:

- Make a list of your top 3 God-given priorities
- Identify 2 things you need to stop doing this week
- Set one new boundary that protects your leadership focus
- Other: ____

Plan it. Do it. Reflect on the result.

Soul Check-Ins

Which of these truths is God emphasizing for you today?

□ My yes needs to serve my purpose
□ Busyness does not equal fruitfulness
□ Focus is a form of obedience
□ When I prioritize heaven's agenda, provision follows

Your Leadership Reminder:
"Effective leaders don't manage time—they steward purpose. Your priorities reveal your prophetic path."

Closing Declaration:

I am a focused leader. I honor my time, my vision, and my calling. I release distraction and align with divine order. Each step I take is intentional. Each decision I make is purposeful. My life and leadership reflect heaven's priorities.

My Notes

Principle #24

The Law of Accountable Leadership

"An unaccountable leader is an unreliable guide."

Scripture Meditation

"So then, each of us will give an account of ourselves to God."

— Romans 14:12

Identity Activation

Accountability is not about control—it's about commitment. As a leader, your willingness to be accountable reveals your level of maturity, integrity, and self-awareness. Leaders who thrive do so not because they answer to no one, but because they humbly submit to trusted voices, spiritual counsel, and wise correction.

In the Kingdom, accountability is a safeguard. It shields you from blind spots and helps you remain aligned with your divine assignment. Being accountable doesn't diminish your authority—it deepens your credibility.

Prompt: *Who have I invited into my life as trusted voices of accountability? What areas of my leadership would benefit from greater transparency?*

Write 3 affirmations that anchor you in accountable leadership:

- I grow in wisdom when I...
- I stay aligned with my calling when I...
- I build trust as a leader when I...

Reflection & Journal Prompt

"Godly leadership doesn't hide behind charisma or titles—it walks humbly in the light."

Prompt:

Accountability invites feedback, correction, and communal growth. It gives others permission to check on you—not just cheer for you.

- What does accountability look like in my leadership practice?
- Am I avoiding hard conversations or feedback that could sharpen me?
- Where do I need to invite deeper accountability in this season?

Now reflect:

What might shift in your relationships if you moved more intentionally towards building on trust, responsibility, and the willingness to be sharpened by others.?

Use the space below to reflect honestly. No filters.

<u>Leadership Practice</u>

This week, choose one area to strengthen your accountability:

- Schedule a check-in with a mentor or spiritual leader
- Ask someone you trust for honest feedback on your leadership
- Identify one area where you need to correct course or realign
- Other: ____

Plan it. Do it. Reflect on the result.

Soul Check-Ins

Which truth resonates most for this principle?

□ I honor God by being accountable for my leadership
□ My growth is multiplied through honest reflection
□ Correction is protection, not rejection
□ I am sharpened by those I trust

Your Leadership Reminder:

"Accountable leaders don't lead alone. They grow through reflection, correction, and godly alignment."

Closing Declaration:

I am a leader who welcomes correction. I walk in truth, not just charisma. I am trusted because I am teachable. I surround myself with wise counsel and refuse to lead in isolation. I grow stronger, wiser, and more impactful through divine accountability.

My Notes

Principle #25

The Law of Creative Leadership

"Leaders who thrive in every season are those who dare to imagine, innovate, and inspire with holy creativity."

Scripture Meditation

"See, I have filled him with the Spirit of God, in wisdom, in understanding, in knowledge, and in all manner of workmanship."
— Exodus 31:3 (NKJV)

Identity Activation

Creativity is not a luxury in leadership—it's a divine necessity. God is the Ultimate Creator, and when He breathed His Spirit into us, He deposited that same creative potential. Whether you're solving a problem, crafting a message, or leading a team, Spirit-led creativity allows you to build, shift, and adapt in ways that honor God and inspire others.

You don't have to be a designer or artist to be creative. Creative leadership shows up in how you communicate vision, design systems, foster collaboration, and approach challenges. It's the difference between doing things the usual way and doing them God's way.

Prompt: *Where have I relied on routine instead of revelation?*
How is God calling me to lead with more creativity in this season?

Write 3 affirmations that stir the creative leader in you:

- I lead with divine imagination when I...
- God has given me creative wisdom to...
- Innovation flows through me because...

Reflection & Journal Prompt

"Creative leadership requires vision, courage, and trust."

Prompt:

Sometimes God gives you a blueprint no one else can see. Your role isn't to shrink back—it's to steward that vision with integrity, even when it hasn't been done before.

- Where have I been boxed in by tradition or fear?
- What fresh idea, approach, or method is God prompting me to activate?

Now reflect:

What might shift in your leadership approach if you activated those creative ideas with boldness?

Use the space below to reflect honestly. No filters.

Leadership Practice

This week, engage your creative leadership by:

- Setting aside 15 minutes to vision cast or brainstorm without limitation
- Solving a current challenge using an unconventional approach
- Asking your team or peers for input on how to creatively improve a process

Plan it. Do it. Reflect on the result.

Soul Check-Ins

Which truth resonates most with you?

□ I reflect the Creator when I lead with vision and bold ideas
□ I don't need to copy—I'm called to create
□ My leadership is enriched by divine wisdom and imagination
□ I bring beauty, strategy, and innovation into every space I enter

Your Leadership Reminder:
"Creative leaders carry heaven's blueprints and birth them in earth's systems."

Closing Declaration:

I am a Spirit-led visionary, anointed to create, adapt, and lead with purpose. God has given me innovative insight and bold ideas to lead in ways that transform lives. I do not lead by default—I lead by design.

My Notes

Principle #26

The Law of Visionary Execution

"A vision without follow-through is just inspiration without transformation."

Scripture Meditation

"Write the vision and make it plain on tablets, that he may run who reads it."
— Habakkuk 2:2 (NKJV)

Identity Activation

God doesn't just give vision for us to dream—He gives it so we'll build. The difference between visionary leaders and passive thinkers is execution. Leaders who shift from talking to building demonstrate faith, courage, and commitment. Execution is where vision becomes impact.

Leadership that stops at ideas never changes lives. God is looking for leaders who will move boldly in faith, strategize with clarity, and take measurable steps toward what He's revealed.

Prompt: *What God-given vision have I delayed putting into action? What's one step I can take this week to move that vision forward?*

Write 3 affirmations that remind you you're not just a dreamer—you're a doer:

- God trusts me to build when I...
- I take ownership of the vision by...
- My next act of obedience is...

Reflection & Journal Prompt

"It's not enough to hear the call—we must move on it."

Prompt:

Execution often means pushing through resistance, doubt, or fear. But remember: partial obedience is still disobedience.

- What systems or support do I need to bring this vision to life?
- How can I simplify my next step so it doesn't feel overwhelming?

Now reflect:

What might shift in your leadership execution if you increased your discipline, clarity, and consistency?

Use the space below to reflect honestly. No filters.

Leadership Practice

This week, lead in visionary execution by:

- Writing or revisiting your short-term vision plan
- Assigning deadlines to at least one key milestone
- Delegating tasks where needed to build sustainable momentum
- Other: ______________________________________

Plan it. Do it. Reflect on the result.

Soul Check-Ins

Which truth resonates most with you?

□ Vision is only powerful when it's acted upon
□ I am responsible for stewarding what God shows me
□ Strategy and discipline are sacred tools in leadership
□ God honors consistent execution, not just big inspiration

Your Leadership Reminder:
"Leaders don't just dream—they design, plan, and deliver."

Closing Declaration:

I am a finisher. I move with clarity, courage, and purpose. God has entrusted me with vision—and I will steward it through action. I am not paralyzed by perfection. I trust Him in the process and take faithful steps forward.

My Notes

Principle #27

The Law of Empowered Belief

"You rise to the level of what you believe is possible—not what others expect."

Scripture Meditation

"As a man thinketh in his heart, so is he."

— Proverbs 23:7 (KJV)

Identity Activation

Empowered leadership starts with empowered belief. What you believe about yourself shapes the limits you break and the legacy you build. If your mindset is bound by fear, insecurity, or small thinking, your leadership will reflect that. But when your belief is rooted in divine identity, the ceiling lifts—and you walk with boldness.

God didn't call you to lead from doubt. He called you to trust His word over your circumstances. The greatest barrier to most visions isn't a lack of resources —it's a lack of belief.

Prompt: *What limiting belief have I been carrying that needs to be surrendered? What would my leadership look like if I fully believed in what God said about me?*

Write down 3 affirmations that help anchor you in empowered belief:

- I trust God's vision for my life even when...
- I rise with boldness when I remember...
- I break limitations by declaring...

Reflection & Journal Prompt

"Leaders who believe in their God-given purpose become immovable."

Prompt:

When you anchor your leadership in belief—not just in yourself, but in the One who sent you—you multiply your impact.

- What promise from God do I need to realign my belief with?
- What would I do differently today if I truly believed I was chosen for this assignment?

Now reflect:

What might shift in your leadership if you aren't shaken by rejection, failure, or opinions?

Use the space below to reflect honestly. No filters.

Leadership Practice

This week, lead with empowered belief by:

- Declaring one scripture over yourself daily
- Replacing every negative thought with a truth from God's word
- Speaking life into another leader who needs a reminder of their worth
- Other: ____

Plan it. Do it. Reflect on the result.

Soul Check-Ins

Which truth resonates most with you?

□ Belief shapes behavior
□ I can't lead others boldly if I doubt my own worth
□ God equips those He calls—so my confidence is in Him
□ Empowered belief is spiritual warfare against fear

Your Leadership Reminder:
"You don't need everyone to believe in you. Just believe what God already said."

Closing Declaration:

I believe I am who God says I am. I silence every lie and lead with faith, not fear. My belief aligns with my purpose, and my mindset is anchored in divine truth. I lead from overflow, not insecurity. I am empowered, chosen, and equipped.

My Notes

Principle #28

The Law of Courageous Communication

"Courageous communication is not about volume—it's about clarity, conviction, and compassion."

Scripture Meditation

"Let your conversation be always full of grace, seasoned with salt, so that you may know how to answer everyone."
— Colossians 4:6

Identity Activation

Leadership isn't just about what you say—it's about how and why you say it. Courageous communication means having the confidence to speak the truth in love, even when it's uncomfortable. It's choosing clarity over confusion, honesty over hiding, and peace over passive-aggression.

Courageous leaders don't avoid hard conversations. They embrace them with maturity, grace, and a desire for growth. Whether in a boardroom, ministry meeting, or kitchen table, they use their words to build—not break.

Prompt: *Where am I holding back my voice because of fear, people-pleasing, or insecurity? What truth do I need to speak this week—with love and wisdom?*

Write 3 affirmations that reinforce your commitment to courageous, grace-filled communication:

- I choose boldness over silence when...
- God's truth flows through me when I...
- My words reflect Heaven's wisdom because...

Reflection & Journal Prompt

"Trust is the cornerstone of leadership"

Prompt:

Think of a recent moment when you withheld your voice or softened your truth to avoid tension. What did that cost you?

- How do I use my words to bring truth, correction, and healing?
- What communication habit is God asking me to refine right now?

Now reflect:

What might shift in your relationships if you communicated with more honesty and care?

Use the space below to reflect honestly. No filters.

Leadership Practice

This week, demonstrate courageous communication by:

- Addressing a necessary but difficult conversation with humility
- Clarifying expectations in a team or relationship setting
- Listening twice as much as you speak—and responding with wisdom
- Other: ___________________________________

Plan it. Do it. Reflect on the result.

Soul Check-Ins

Which area of communication is God highlighting for refinement?

□ Speaking up when I normally shrink back
□ Being more clear, not just kind
□ Leading hard conversations with truth and grace
□ Listening deeply before I respond

Your Leadership Reminder:
"Your voice is a vessel for change. Don't let fear mute what Heaven is calling you to speak."

Closing Declaration:

I will not shrink back from difficult truths. I speak with clarity, wisdom, and authority. My words are rooted in grace, and I use my voice to bring peace, correction, and impact. I lead with courageous communication that reflects God's heart.

My Notes

Principle #29

The Law of Mutual Growth

"Leaders grow when they help others grow. Leadership is not a solo climb —it's a shared ascent."

Scripture Meditation

"As iron sharpens iron, so one person sharpens another."
— Proverbs 27:17

Identity Activation

True leadership thrives in community. The Law of Mutual Growth reminds us that we are not meant to grow alone—nor should we. Growth is magnified when it's shared, multiplied, and nurtured in relationship with others.

Whether in ministry, the marketplace, or education, leaders must resist the temptation to hoard wisdom or guard their success. Instead, they intentionally invest in others while remaining open to growth themselves. In a culture that often celebrates individualism, mutual growth invites us to embrace collaboration, vulnerability, and shared transformation.

Prompt: *Who in your life stretches and sharpens you as a leader? How can you be more intentional about growing with others this season?*

Write 3 affirmations that center your leadership around mutual growth and shared purpose:

- I grow stronger when I...
- My leadership multiplies when I...
- I welcome the wisdom of others because...

Reflection & Journal Prompt

"God's model has always been teams—not titles."

Prompt:

Think about a time when collaboration with another person made your work or leadership better. How did that connection challenge and grow you?

- Am I surrounding myself with people who sharpen and stretch me?
- Do I create space for others to grow in my presence?
- Where is God calling me to release the need to "lead alone"?

Now reflect:

What might shift in your relationships if you released control and opened yourself up to more opportunities to collaborate?

Use the space below to reflect honestly. No filters.

<u>Leadership Practice</u>

This week, activate mutual growth by:

- Seeking feedback from someone you trust
- Offering guidance or mentorship to a peer or team member
- Praying for a divine partnership that will elevate your leadership journey
- Other: ______________________________________

Plan it. Do it. Reflect on the result.

Soul Check-Ins

Where are you being invited to grow with someone, not just around them?

□ Mentorship (receiving or giving)
□ Collaborative projects
□ Being teachable in unfamiliar territory
□ Building new leadership friendships

Your Leadership Reminder:
"Leadership isn't about climbing faster—it's about reaching higher together."

Closing Declaration:

"I embrace mutual growth as a leadership strategy and Kingdom principle. I grow by helping others rise, and I rise through the wisdom and support of those around me. I am sharpened, stretched, and strengthened by community—and I willingly pour into others as I continue to grow."

My Notes

Principle #30

The Law of Authentic Acceptance

"You cannot lead what you do not accept. True leadership begins with seeing people as they are—fully and completely—and leading them with grace."

Scripture Meditation

"Accept one another, then, just as Christ accepted you, in order to bring praise to God."
— Romans 15:7

Identity Activation

Authentic acceptance isn't passive—it's a leadership choice. It's the intentional act of embracing others with grace, humility, and spiritual maturity. Leaders who practice this principle don't overlook faults, but they don't weaponize them either. They hold space for others to grow while reflecting Christlike compassion in their leadership approach.

Acceptance doesn't mean agreement. It means you see the person beyond their role, their past, or their current struggle. It creates an environment of safety, allowing others to show up fully, be seen, and thrive. As leaders, we mirror God's acceptance of us when we create space for others to belong.

Prompt: *Who has modeled authentic acceptance in your life? Are there people you lead that you need to see with fresh eyes?*

Write 3 affirmations about your ability to lead with authentic acceptance:

- I reflect God's love when I...
- My leadership becomes a safe place when I...
- I lead people well when I see them as...

Reflection & Journal Prompt

"Self-awareness is the first step toward acceptance."

Prompt:

Think about a time you felt fully accepted by someone in leadership or spiritual authority. How did it change you?

How can you replicate that atmosphere for those you lead?

- Do I place conditions on who I choose to affirm or invest in?
- What internal biases might be blocking my ability to lead others with grace?
- How can I shift my leadership posture to reflect more of God's heart?

Now reflect:

What might shift in your relationships if you embraced authentic acceptance?

Use the space below to reflect honestly. No filters.

Leadership Practice

This week, activate authentic acceptance by:

- Listening to someone without correcting or judging
- Praying for God to reveal hidden biases in your leadership
- Intentionally affirming someone you've overlooked or misunderstood
- Other: ____

Plan it. Do it. Reflect on the result.

Soul Check-Ins

Where might God be calling you to lead with greater acceptance?

□ Within your leadership team
□ Toward a difficult personality
□ In how you view your own past
□ In making space for diverse perspectives

Your Leadership Reminder:
"Leadership shaped by acceptance creates culture shaped by love."

Closing Declaration:

I accept others with the same grace God extended to me. I do not lead from superiority, but from humility, compassion, and authenticity. I create space for people to grow without shame and thrive without fear. Acceptance is not weakness—it is Kingdom strength, and I carry it well.

My Notes

Principle #31

The Law of Empowering Embrace

"When leaders embrace others with empowerment, they don't just welcome them—they lift them. True leadership creates space for others to rise."

Scripture Meditation

"Encourage one another and build each other up, just as in fact you are doing."
— 1 Thessalonians 5:11

Identity Activation

Empowering embrace is more than encouragement—it's an invitation to rise. Great leaders don't cling to their own influence; they extend it. They see potential in others, name it, nurture it, and release it with intentionality. To empower someone is to trust them with responsibility, voice, and vision.

When a leader embraces others with empowerment, they shift from competition to collaboration, from control to community. They don't just open the door—they walk with others through it. That embrace becomes a mantle—a tangible sign of trust, value, and spiritual alignment.

Prompt: *Who has empowered you through their embrace of your gifts or purpose? Who are you called to lift as you lead?*

Write 3 affirmations that align with your call to empower others through your leadership:

- I create impact by...
- I see the God-given potential in others and...
- I embrace others not to control, but to...

Reflection & Journal Prompt

The embrace that empowers says,
"You belong. You matter. You can lead too."

Prompt:

Think about someone who is under your influence—a peer, mentee, student, team member, or even a child. How can your words, posture, or actions offer them a sense of empowerment today?

- Am I leading with a heart that releases or one that restricts?
- Where have I withheld affirmation or opportunities because of insecurity or control?
- How can I better model servant leadership that lifts others?

Now reflect:

What might shift in your relationships if you demonstrated the power of embrace by seeing yourself as someone worthy of acceptance?

Use the space below to reflect honestly. No filters.

Leadership Practice

This week, activate empowering embrace by:

- Delegating a meaningful responsibility to someone ready to grow
- Publicly acknowledging another's contribution
- Praying intentionally for someone under your leadership to rise in boldness
- Other: ____

Plan it. Do it. Reflect on the result.

Soul Check-Ins

What might God be calling you to release in order to empower others?

□ Control over outcomes
□ Fear of being replaced
□ The need for constant recognition
□ Perfectionism or micromanagement

Your Leadership Reminder (Write your own):
"When you lead with empowerment, your legacy lives in those you've lifted."

Closing Declaration:

I lead with open hands and an open heart. I do not shrink from sharing my influence, but embrace others with the intent to raise them. I create space for growth, voice, and bold steps of faith. My leadership leaves room for others to rise, for Kingdom expansion requires many hands, not just mine.

My Notes

YOU DID IT!

I pray you've Activated a deeper knowing of your God-given identity, Imparted new wisdom through each law, and felt the divine permission to Release old limitations, old fears, and outdated frameworks that no longer serve you.
You were never meant to lead on empty.

You were never meant to dim your light to match the room.
You were never meant to do it alone.

Now go forward: refilled, reawakened, and re-aligned. Multiply the message. Walk boldly in your assignment.
And remember:

The world needs what's in you.

Breathe deep. Then lead well.
Amen and amen.

Dr. Ansonya

WANT TO KEEP GOING?

GET MY RESOURCES !

If your soul is hungry or if you're in need of motivation, guidance and inspiration - physically, mentally and spiritually, look no further! We've got many tools available and we're making them available to you. Explore each product and find just the right thing to give your soul the fuel it desperately needs.

I work with an honest and caring approach to assist you in navigating through life's Expectations, Pressures and Challenges. From my many years of experience as an international life design coach, I have come to understand the psychology behind what makes people tick, what makes them succumb to societal pressures and what makes them feed their ambitions when they needed to feed their spirits.

WWW.ANSONYABURKE.ORG

WWW.ANSONYABURKE.ORG

WWW.ANSONYABURKE.ORG

GET THE BOOK & SCHEDULE A CONSULTATION

LET'S WORK TOGETHER

USING SCIENTIFICALLY PROVEN METHODS

I CAN HELP YOU UNLOCK YOUR FULL POTENTIAL.

There is a generation of leaders and progressive thinkers that are roaming this earth searching for someone who will give them permission to live beyond the barriers of the box.

There are leaders who are anxiously sitting on the sidelines of purpose, hoping and waiting that someone will come along to launch them into the unique greatness that they sense is associated with their life.

Discover the simple 3 Steps that I Discovered to Hack Productivity. It works 100%.

LEAVE DR. BURKE YOUR

REVIEW

We hope you enjoyed this experience and found lots of value to support your leadership journey!

We would appreciate it if you wouldn't mind taking the time to leave Dr. Burke a review.

You can go to **Amazon.com** or **AnsonyaBurke.org** (under "contacts") and submit your review.

Thanks!

Dr. Ansonya L. Burke

THANK YOU FOR YOUR FEEDBACK!

Made in the USA
Coppell, TX
10 January 2026

65279613R10074